BOOI

Writ

Translate

Antigone

BY JEAN ANOUILH

BrightSummaries.com

13987

Composition
NORD COMPO

Achevé d'imprimer à Barcelone
par CPI Black Print
le 3 décembre 2023

Dépôt légal décembre 2023
EAN 9782290381298
OTP L21EPLN003385-548192

ÉDITIONS J'AI LU
82, rue Saint-Lazare, 75009 Paris

Diffusion France et étranger : Flammarion

www.brightsummaries.com

Ebook EAN: 9782806294760

Paperback EAN: 9782806294777

Legal Deposit: D/2015/12603/457

Cover: © Primento

Digital conception by Primento, the digital partner of publishers.

Printed in Great Britain
by Amazon

47863298R00020

JEAN ANOUILH

FRENCH WRITER AND PLAYWRIGHT

- **Born in Bordeaux in 1910**
- **Died in Lausanne in 1987**
- **Notable works:**
    - *The Traveller Without Luggage* (1937), play
    - *Thieves' Carnival* (1938), comedy
    - *Antigone* (1942), tragedy

A discreet man, Jean Anouilh first began working for an advertising agency. But in 1928, a performance of Jean Giraudoux's *Siegfried* convinced him to write for the theater. In 1930, he became the secretary of Louis Jouvet (French actor and director, 1887-1951; Director at the Athenaeum Theatre). Given their incompatible personalities, this collaboration turned out to be a short one. However, this experience prompted him to write *L'Hermine* (1932). His inspirations, besides Marivaux and Musset which he 'read a thousand times', were as diverse as Claudel, Pirandello, Shaw and Molière.

A prolific playwright, he classified his plays, all marked with deep pessimism, according to categories with revelatory titles: 'black' plays (*Antigone*, 1944) 'pink' plays (*Thieves' Carnival*, 1938), 'grating' plays (*The Cave*, 1961), 'brilliant' plays (*Repetition*, 1950), 'costumed' plays (*The Lark*, 1953), 'secret' plays (*The Arrest*, 1975) and even 'joker' plays (*The Navel*, 1981).

ANTIGONE

A FAMOUS TRAGEDY

- **Genre:** Tragedy
- **Reference edition:** Anouilh, J. (1975) *Antigone*. Paris: La Table Ronde.[1]
- **First edition:** 1944
- **Themes:** tragedy, family, respect, prohibition

Antigone is a modern tragedy written in prose, adapted from the ancient text of Sophocles. Published in 1944 under the Occupation, the play was approved by Nazi censorship, which viewed Creon's victory as a justification of the established order. After an initially cold reception, the play experienced huge success. This is probably due to the fact that the youth interpreted the author's intentions differently than the Nazi occupiers and admired the heroine for daring to stand up to authority, instead of seeing the play as an acceptation of the power in place.

The many anachronisms in the play, and the fact that it is presented in the form of a continuous dialogue, without any formal division, separate it from traditional French theater.

Even today, the play is the subject of extraordinary interest. All idealists can identify with Antigone's search for purity and the absolute.

1. Quotes taken from the reference edition have been translated by BrightSummaries.com.

SUMMARY

TRANSGRESSION

The niece of Creon, King of Thebes, Antigone, enters the palace at dawn after burying her brother, Polynices, despite the official ban announced by her uncle promising death to all those who violated the law. She reassures her nurse, who is worried about the behavior of her beloved girl, by hiding the truth from her. In turn, the nurse tries to comfort Antigone who is vulnerable and seeks a form of childish comfort.

Antigone also hides her actions from her older sister, Ismene, who is worried when she realizes that her sister is planning to bury her brother despite the royal decree: she doesn't yet know that Antigone has already done it. Despite their tender dialogue, rivalry between the two women soon comes to light. Antigone also demands that Haemon, her fiancé and son of Creon, promises to abstain from asking her any questions about her refusal to marry him, after which she asks him to leave.

When Antigone returns to her sister, she tries to convince Ismene not to go and bury Polynices, arguing that her brother never liked her: Antigone later tells her that it has already been done.

CONFESSION

A guard tells Creon that Polynices' body has been partially

covered with earth. The king chooses to avoid scandal by having the guard and his companions sworn to secrecy about the act of rebellion. However, Antigone is caught covering Polynice's body with earth, finishing what she had begun that night. The guards lead her to the king who, in disbelief, finds his niece in handcuffs. From then on, Creon does all he can to prevent her death.

First, he offers to sweep the issue under the rug, under the pretense that it was but a childish whim, but Antigone retorts that she was fully aware of what she was doing and she will only do it again if Creon releases her. He then exposes the absurdity of the religious rites, but she says that she only did it 'for her'. Creon explains to her the difficulty of ruling and the political and social reasons that obliged him to publish the decree. He asks her to understand him, but Antigone refuses to listen: "I do not want to understand...I am here to say no to you and to die."

THE FATES

So, Creon, in a final attempt to convince her, reveals the true story of his two unworthy brothers "who were slaughtered like the two little thugs they were, for a settling of accounts...". This time, Antigone wavers on learning that Polynices was just "a stupid little party animal, a little carnivore, hard and soulless", even towards their father, Oedipus, who she respected. Creon, wanting to claim his victory, gives her the definition of happiness, at which point Antigone turns into the young rebellious girl she has always been and shatters Creon's reasoning: "You disgust me with

all your happiness." "As for me, I want everything now and whole - or else I refuse!", she exclaims, showing stubborn, even blind, logic without any chance of compromise.

At this moment, Ismene arrives and offers to die along with her sister. Antigone refuses, claiming it is too late: "Do not think you can die with me now. It would be too easy.", she asserts, referring to one of their exchanges, when Ismene refused to suffer. Infuriated by Antigone's provocative behavior, Creon gives up on saving her and calls his guards. "Finally", she cries: she will die fulfilling her destiny, her fate.

Creon must then endure the protests of the Chorus, which he rejects: "It was she who wanted to die. None of us were strong enough to persuade her to live." He then remains immovable in the face of Haemon's desperate attempts to save his bride, by putting himself on the side of the law and his role as king: "I am the master before the law. Not after." Meanwhile, alone with a guard, Antigone dictates him a letter to be given to Haemon, in which she confesses: "I no longer know why I am dying..."

THE DEATH OF ANTIGONE

It is the messenger who announces the terrible news. Antigone, condemned to be entombed alive, has chosen to hang herself in her tomb with her belt, so as to spare the city her sullied blood. Arriving too late, Haemon throws himself into the lifeless arms of his fiancée. Arriving on the scene, Creon tries to lift up his son who no longer hears him. Haemon gets up and spits in his face, then "looks at him with his childlike eyes, heavy with contempt", before

plunging his sword into his own stomach.

The messenger finally announces the death of Eurydice, Creon's wife, who silently slit her own throat on learning of her son's death. Creon is left alone, with only his page. He is going to attend council, because he is the king. As for the guards, "it is none of their business, they continue to play cards".

CHARACTER STUDY

ANTIGONE

In the prologue, Anouilh describes her as:

- Physically, a "young dark-haired girl", "small [and] lean", with "serious eyes" and a "sad smile", "her arms around her knees";
- Morally, she is a dreamer and "withdrawn": "No one in the family takes her seriously."

Thus, Antigone is not what you might call a beautiful woman, unlike her sister. He also says that she is "not beautiful like us, but in a different way", which implies that Antigone has a unique kind of beauty. Even her nurse who adores her says: "My God, this little one is not very pretty". Her beauty therefore comes from within.

Her unfavorable physique, like a "sparrow", as Creon tells her, is coupled with the gravity and sadness reflected in her eyes and smile. The fetal position further accentuates her physical-moral uneasiness, a characteristic of isolation, her introversion and her need for security. This position is a prelude to her true birth: she will leave it to "stand alone against the world".

Therefore, the real Antigone attracts people with her personality, which Creon describes as being "the pride of Oedipus", adding that "human misfortune, it was not enough". As a matter of fact, Antigone admits, short of

arguments against her uncle, that this act of burying her brother had been done "for no-one", but for herself. With this assertion, she claims her complete freedom even though, facing death, she becomes aware of her loneliness ("all alone") and fears ("I no longer know why I am dying. I am afraid..."). She is drawn to death as the sublime conclusion of an oversized ideal, but in the end it frightens her.

Antigone is a rebel, and has been since her childhood. She pushes this rebellion to its limits in her dialogue with Creon: "I do not want to understand...I am here to say no to you and to die."; "You disgust me with all your happiness!"; "As for me, I want everything now and whole - or else I refuse!"

These three sentences spoken by Antigone are real provocations that will push Creon to uphold her death sentence. The last quote is perhaps the one that best characterizes the girl; full of integrity, refusing compromise, but unfortunately on that occasion also confused about the difference between making a compromise and compromising oneself.

She is thus idealistic and full of integrity, but with an excessive idealism that will cost her life.

Yet, Antigone has a true passion for life, real life. She loves to get up early at dawn: "It is a beautiful garden that doesn't yet think of men"; "Who got up first in the morning, just to feel the cold air on her bare skin?"; But like all passionate people, she is eternally unsatisfied. She cannot appreciate happiness because she is scared of the next moment. So she tells Haemon: "When you think that I will be yours, do you feel a huge hole inside you that widens, as if something were

dying?". This sentence may also be explained by Antigone's acceptance of her tragic fate. As heiress of the Labdacides family, she knows her destiny can only lie in the fulfillment of her family's curse. Thus, she will remain faithful to Oedipus, her father, out of filial loyalty: "Yes, I am ugly! ... Father did not become beautiful until later, when he had finally had the complete certainty that he had indeed killed his father, that it was indeed his mother with whom he had slept, and that nothing, nothing at all could save him." This loyalty can also be seen in her desperate act of burying her brother.

Antigone is also, despite being 20, a little girl, who uses a small shovel to cover Polynices' body, the same she and her brother used to build sandcastles. She is a very young, fragile girl, as shown in the scene with her nurse where she seeks her warmth and her hand, in order to no longer be afraid "of the wicked ogre". She is a fierce creature who mourns her childhood: "I want to be sure of everything to-day and have it as beautiful as when I was little - or to die", because that was a time of purity and innocence. Antigone is a permanent and eternal antimony.

CREON

In the prologue, Anouilh describes him as:

- Physically, a "strong man" with "white hair". "He [also] has wrinkles" and "[...] is tired";
- Morally, he is the king. "He plays the difficult game of leading men. Before, he loved "music, fine bookbinding",

> but since he became king, "he has rolled up his sleeves. In the morning, he gets up, quiet, like a worker at the threshold of his day".

Anouilh presents Creon as a worn and tired man who never expected to reign. The deaths of Oedipus and his two sons gave him access to the royal power, a task for which he was not prepared, but will perform as best he can: "One morning I woke up King of Thebes. And God knows I liked many other things in life than being powerful." Undoubtedly conscientious, he is, however, more hard-working than ambitious:

> "I am just Creon, thank God. I have both feet on the ground, both hands in my pockets and, since I am king, I have decided, with less ambition than your father, to simply dedicate myself to making the order of this world a little less absurd, if possible."

By this phrase, he admits his lack of audacity. In the name of common sense, he advocates accommodation while he admits that he used to have other ideas: "I heard from the depths of time a young Creon, thin and pale like you, and like you he could think of nothing else but giving everything." Thus, he considers himself like Antigone, who would not have gone through with her fate, which his niece criticizes during their long conversation.

This long discussion between the uncle and his niece, the real cornerstone of Anouilh's tragedy, symbolizes the impossible encounter between two diametrically opposed visions of the world, that of the law and that of conscience.

During this dialogue, Creon shows great patience and benevolent, almost paternal, understanding. However, confronted with the repeated provocations of Antigone and listening to his sense of duty, he condemns her to death. The "young Creon, thin and pale, who could think of nothing else but giving everything" is completely overtaken by his royal duty. He becomes the agent of power again, a kind of anti-hero in the service of human law.

On his own throughout the play, and as the sole decider of Antigone's fate, his loneliness appears most evidently at the end. The Chorus also makes the comment to him, "And you're all alone now, Creon." In fact, as his whole family is wiped out following the suicides of Haemon, his son, and Eurydice, his wife, he finds himself more alone than ever.

ISMENE

In the prologue, Anouilh describes her as:

- Physically, "blond", "beautiful", "happy" and "sensual";
- Morally, she "chats and laughs", "has a "taste for dance and games" and a "taste for happiness and success".

What is surprising in the prologue is that Ismene is the only character not to be presented individually. She is only mentioned in relation to Antigone and Haemon.

Thus, Ismene is a character who is defined by comparison, either through her affinities with Haemon, or in contrast to Antigone. In fact, everything is different about the two sisters, physically and morally. The reflection and prudence of

the older sister clash with the passion and prudent audacity of the younger sister. The phrase "I somewhat understand our uncle" said by Ismene, is followed by "I do not want to understand somewhat" said by Antigone. When Ismene says "Listen to me, I'm right more often than you", Antigone responds by saying "I do not want to be right", which shows her determination and stubbornness.

The two female characters of the play are, therefore, completely different. Ismene is a beautiful, sensual young woman looking for simple and material happiness, with a "taste for dance and games [...] happiness and success". This type of happiness is specifically rejected by Antigone, with all her boyish determination.

The excerpt that is most revealing of Ismene's personality appears in her dialogue with Antigone. From the beginning of the conversation, Ismene reports twice that she has "thought it through well" before saying three times that she "thinks". This emphasis indicates that Ismene acts based on reason, unlike Antigone who is guided by her passion, but it may also indicate a lack of confidence since Ismene finds it necessary to state five times her "thinking" and to support this three times using the adverb "well". Then, Ismene shows perfect mastery of dialectic by alternating logical and psychological arguments. Wanting to convince her sister of the absurdity of her gesture, she first tries to reason with her, then, when this has no effect, she changes her strategy by trying to speak to her heart. The construction of her speech is proof that she is a thoughtful person. We can also observe that Antigone never tries to disprove her sister's arguments,

she only responds using negative sentences and thus refuses to enter into a real discussion.

ANALYSIS

If there was ever a play that has raised, and still raises, controversy, it is Anouilh's *Antigone*. But why is there so much controversy?

ANTIGONE AND THE RESISTANCE

The controversy regarding *Antigone* is the natural consequence of the context in which the play was written. Indeed, it was written in Paris in 1942, when it was occupied by German troops, a few weeks after the attack of a young French Resistant, Paul Collette, against collaborators, including Pierre Laval and Marcel Déat, who were left wounded. Many have seen and still see that act as a form of useless heroism that might have inspired Anouilh to create the character of Antigone.

THE AUTHOR'S POINT OF VIEW

However, we should be cautious and remember only what Anouilh himself wrote concerning his motivations for writing this play. "On the day of the little 'Affiches rouges', I rediscovered with a sudden shock the *Antigone* of Sophocles, which I had read and re-read countless times and had practically always known by heart'. I rewrote it in my own way, with the resonance of the tragedy we were all going through." These 'affiches rouges' (which inspired the famous poem by Aragon in praise of the Resistance) plastered all over France by the Vichy regime and the Nazis, were exploiting the execution of 23 resistants, whom the Nazis

tried to pass off to the French people as terrorists. Without denying the influence of its historical context, Anouilh therefore does not refer to the act of Paul Collette.

Anouilh's statement also raises a problem. How could he have been inspired by these 'affiches rouges' that appeared in 1944 when he wrote the play in 1942 and it was performed from 1944 onwards? Some claim he didn't remember the chronology with precision. Others take advantage of this to reaffirm that the senseless act of Paul Collette was definitely the trigger of the play.

CONSCIENCE VS. LAW

Another controversial element is the fact that, during certain performances, Anouilh and Barsacq (designer and theater director, 1909-1973) distributed leaflets encouraging the Resistance, whereas the same Resistance accused Anouilh of collaboration and some clandestine circles even threatened him. As you recall, Nazi censorship agreed to the text's release, perceiving Antigone's death as Creon's victory and thus the victory of the established order, and that it was the youth who, perceiving the death of Antigone as the triumph of purity and the refusal to compromise with 'the enemy', made it a huge success. Consequently, Anouilh's *Antigone* also symbolizes generational conflict. On the one side, we observe Creon the adult, the rational man looking for a modus vivendi that would be a synthesis of middle ground solutions, and on the other side, Antigone, the embodiment of a youth who is driven by a quest for the absolute and an opposition to the world as it is. This antagonism, particu-

larly present in the dialogues between Antigone and Creon, is at the heart of this impossible midpoint between two conceptions of duty: Antigone's duty to her conscience and Creon's duty to the law.

A DETAILED CONTROVERSY

The fact that the guards play cards in leather coats is reminiscent of the Gestapo and has appealed to the people's emotions, all the more so because Anouilh does not sit in judgment of their behavior, despite its roughness and animal-like characteristic: "These guys are not bad..." But these guards in leather jackets "are the auxiliaries of Creon's justice". We can now understand the dubious amalgam that is created in the minds of some spectators and the resulting controversy. Do not forget that the play was written in the late summer of 1942, i.e. just weeks after the roundup of thousands of French Jews in the Vel d'Hiv for their deportation to concentration camps or extermination camps. The lack of judgment from these "officers of Creon's court" dressed in leather jackets could therefore be logically interpreted as a form of acceptance of the established order.

POLITICAL SIGNIFICANCE

The political significance of the play can be directly linked to the controversy related to the motivation at the origin of its writing. However, we have just seen that it is necessary to keep some distance and remain cautious as to the motives that allegedly led Anouilh to compose his tragedy.

Does this mean that Anouilh would have written his play driven solely by his growing interest in classic culture? This does not seem plausible since many objective elements of the tragedy come together with an Antigone allegory of the Resistance, through her fierce opposition to the established power, and Creon personifying the acceptance of the Occupation.

A cautious conclusion about the controversy and the political significance of the works would therefore involve recognizing the influence of the historical context of the time, something that Anouilh has also readily accepted, without interpreting too freely the elements that could equally be analyzed as the complete opposite. For example, although idolized by an idealistic youth, for Anouilh, Antigone is nothing but an "ungrateful and arrogant little girl like those of May '68!" Similarly, although, in the eyes of some, the heroine Antigone overcomes the compromised power through her death, she admits that she no longer knows why she is dying, leading both a Haemon in love, who could have lived happily at her side, and a Eurydice completely broken by her son's suicide into the darkness.

FURTHER REFLECTION

SOME QUESTIONS TO THINK ABOUT...

- Compare the characters of Ismene and Antigone.
- Compare Anouilh's *Antigone* to Sophocles' (Greek tragic poet, circa 496-406BC) by linking the differences between the two works to the historical and political context of the time, and by examining the very different religious approaches of the authors.
- Also compare Anouilh's and Bauchau's (Belgian writer, 1913-2012) representations of the character of Antigone.
- Establish a parallel between the dialogue between Antigone and Ismene and the dialogue between Antigone and Creon. What do you notice?
- Anouilh highlights, in the dialogue between Antigone and Creon, a conceit (an extended metaphor or a succession of metaphors on the same theme). Analyze this.
- "I am the master before the law. Not after." Comment on this remark by Creon.
- Creon is faced with a terrible dilemma. What is it? Is it comparable to those that tear apart the characters of Racine (French tragic poet, 1639-1699) or Corneille (French dramatic poet, 1606-1684)?
- Anouilh's play represents two radically opposed visions of the world: that of the law and that of conscience. Explain what these two visions involve.
- This play is part of the 'black' plays by Anouilh. Justify this classification.
- What do you think of Antigone's attitude? Do you think it is worth dying for your ideas? Argue your case by using

famous historical examples.

We want to hear from you!
Leave a comment on your online library
and share your favourite books on social media!

FURTHER READING

REFERENCE EDITION

- Anouilh, J. (1975) *Antigone*. Paris: La Table Ronde.

REFERENCE STUDIES

- De Comminges, É. (1977) *Anouilh, littérature et politique*. Saint-Genouph: Nizet.
- Mitterand, H. (1992) *Dictionnaire des grandes œuvres de la littérature française*. Paris: Le Robert.